The Magick of Saint Expedite

Tap into The Truly Miraculous Power Of Saint Expedite

Copyright information

Kadmon, Baal

The Magick of Saint Expedite - Tap Into The Truly Miraculous Power Of Saint Expedite

—1st ed

Printed in the United States of America

Cover image : Wellcome Library, London [CC BY 4.0 (httpcreativecommons.orglicensesby4.0)], via Wikimedia Commons

Book Cover Design: Baal Kadmon

Dedication

This book is dedicated to the great Saint Expedite. He has always provided in times of need. May your name be exalted upon the Earth.

Introduction

From all the saints to work with , Saint Expedite is the most responsive. It is for this reason I am writing this book with great enthusiasm. Saint Expedite works very quickly. He is always ready to help. **He has helped thousands upon thousands of people overcome financial hardships.** If you do an internet search, you will find thousands upon thousands of testimonials about him. He truly is a miracle worker.(I will provide various links at the end of this book.)

Saint Expedite works so well that I felt compelled to publish a work about this great saint and provide you all the information you will need to tap into his miraculous power. On a personal level, Whenever I have been in financial binds, Saint Expedite always came through. ALWAYS! He comes through for thousands of others every day, all over the world. No matter what your personal belief is, he will work for you too.

Saint Expedite has a rich history in the magickal community, especially Hoodoo and voodoo communities. Working with Saint Expedite is in a real sense performing saint Magick which is a backbone of the Hoodoo Magickal Tradition.

In this book, we will cover who Saint Expedite is and how to tap into his power. Before that, however, we will discuss, in brief, Saint Magick in general.

Saint Magick -The Hoodoo Connection

(Excerpted from Mary Magick)

What is Hoodoo?

Hoodoo is known by many names, most popularly as " Conjure" or : Rootworking". It is a considered to a folk magical tradition that weaves, European, Native American and West African elements together. Hoodoo is believed to originate in Mississippi and was formulated by the slaves working on the plantations at the time. In time, it spread. You can find the hub of Hoodoo in New Orleans. The beauty of Hoodoo is that it is synergistic; it evolves and incorporates many otherwise disparate spiritual traditions together. Despite this, there is a clear presence of Christian Saints in its spiritual practices. At first, the Africans who were harshly brought here as slaves still believed in traditional West African spirituality that was mostly nature based but also had a concept of supreme creator with a pantheon of lesser-known but highly venerated deities. This tradition had a heavy reliance on charms and spells. In time, as Christianity seeped into the overall population, much, but NOT all, of the old beliefs were replaced. What was not replaced, was incorporated with the new Christian beliefs. A belief that truly impacted was the clear idea of good and evil. This would later inform the magickal spells that would develop in Hoodoo.

As the ideas melded further, everything became cast in the light of Hoodoo. God became a Hoodoo doctor and created the universe through magick. Moses the liberator of the Israelites in the book of Exodus was considered a Conjurer because he used intention and divine power to produce the miracles that he did. In many ways, all of us who practice magick are Hoodoo Doctors aren't we?

In the Hoodoo tradition the bible took on a new role. It was not just a holy book anymore but a book of magick or " Conjure". Especially the Psalms which formed the basis for a rich magickal tradition. We will cover Psalms Magick in another book. In general, the bible became essentially a talisman unto its own.

Like all Practitioners of Magick of all traditions, the point of Magick is to bring something into being via supernatural means. Something that will improve either our own lives and the lives of others.

We will now discuss the great Saint Expedite.

Saint Expedite - The Miracle Worker

Saint Expedite, also known as Expeditus was born in Armenia. It is not clear when he was born, but it is known that he died a Martyr in 303 A.D in Melitene Turkey .

According to Catholic traditions, Saint Expedite was a Roman Centurion who was based out in Armenia. He was initially a pagan but later converted to Christianity, as many Roman Soldiers did. His conversion was to eventually lead to his death during the Diocletian Persecution of Christians in 303 A.D. Before his conversion, it is said that the devil came to him in a form of a crow and encouraged him to put off his conversion until the following day. Saint expedite refused and crushed the bird under his feet and killed it. He thus declared, " I will be Christian today!" This is important to make note of because the typical iconography of Saint expedite depicts him stomping on a bird that is saying "CRAS" which means "tomorrow" in Latin. Saint Expedite then lifts a cross with the word " Hodie" engraved in it. Hodie being the word for "Today"

This fact also gives him the reputation as working very quickly on peoples requests. He doesn't wait, he works on them TODAY.

Saint Expedite was declared a martyr in 1781, in Italy where his cult survived in Turin since the middle ages. He was called upon for his rapid response when settling legal issues and financial troubles. he is still quite popular in Europe and very much so in Latin America. On April 19th ,Saint Expedites feast day, Sao Paolo, Brazil erupts in celebration.

As with so many mysterious saintly figures, the stories behind Saint Expedite is shrouded in mystery.

As with all mysteries, they are often accompanied by many folk stories. Many revolve around him. Some have said that the term Expeditus is not actually his real name but a misnomer.

The story takes place in France, 1781, a shipment of relics arrived , many were unidentified. However, on the box containing his statute, the word "Expedite" was marked on the package. Some believed it simply meant that the package was to be expedited to its final location whereas others believed that was the name of the Saint whose statue was contained in the package. When Nuns at the

Denfret-Rochereau Catcombs in Paris saw this, they prayed to this "unknown" saint and the prayers were all answered. Word of this quickly spread and the miracles of Saint Expedite would spread throughout the Catholic world and beyond.

Another version of this story takes place far from France, but in New Orleans. In this version, (no doubt influenced by the French story since the French colonized New Orleans) a shipment of relics arrived at the Chapel of Our Lady of Guadalupe. As with the French story, one package had no other marking except the term " Expedit". And thus, he was known to the locals as Saint Expedite. New Orleans, like Brazil still venerates Saint Expedite to this day. He is very prominent in Creole Folklore.

Other pockets of veneration exist such as in Chile and the French Island Of Reunion. In Chile, he is known as "San Expedito", it is said that a devotee arrived to Chile with his statute. She asked local priests to erect a church to him. Eventually the church was built and until this day, he is worshiped and is very popular in Chile. In Chile they say a special prayer to Saint Expedite:

A thousand hymns to glorious Expeditus,

Who shed his blood in Armenia,

Whose name was written in heaven,

And gained the laurel of martyrdom.

—Hymn to Saint Expeditus

Source: Vilagrán, Ángel Rodríguez. "San Expedito". *El Ángel de la Web*

Although we will not use this prayer in our rituals, it can't hurt to keep it in mind. It is quite beautiful.

In the Reunion Islands, like the other stories speak of a package of relics with the name Expedite on it. However, in Reunion it seems that worshiping Saint Expedite publically is considered a taboo, but that doesn't stop people from secretly worshiping him since it appears small shrines to him are still maintained.

As you can see, not much is known about his life, but **one thing is for sure. He listens to prayers.** Although one can simply pray to him, his Novena card is found in Many Churches, there does seem to be consensus as to the best way to call upon him. In the next chapter we will discuss the most popular ways to call upon him. Following that, we will discuss more in-depth on how to call upon him.

Saint Expedite Magick - The Basics

What you will need to call upon Saint Expedite.

1. A Statue or printed image of him. A Novena Card works too. I have this statute of Saint Expedite:

<u>12" Inch Saint Expedite Figurine</u>

Or you can use Novena cards, This is the one I have on one of my altars.

<u>Holy Prayer Cards For the Prayer to Saint Expedite In English</u>

2. 7 day - Red Candles - Any 7 day Red Candles will do.

3. A glass of Water

<u>**All these will be placed on the Altar. I will show you how to setup the altar momentarily.**</u>

In general, the best day to call upon Saint Expedite is on Wednesday for it is the day of Mercury who was the messenger God in the Roman Pantheon.

<u>VERY IMPORTANT:</u>

When he grants your request, You MUST give him an offering. If you don't, he can take away everything he has given you and then some. You can give one or all of these offerings to Saint Expedite when he completes your favor. However, the last item is A MUST.

Most common offerings are:

5 pennies. I give 5 quarters, it just seems right to me.

5 pieces of pound cake. Any brand will do but some folk legends say Sarah Lees is best. I for one use any I can find. I like using the Small hand sized cakes.

A Red Rose

A Glass of Red Wine

And perhaps most importantly, you MUST announce to the world that Saint Expedite helped you. If you have a blog you can do it there. You can also create a YouTube video as well since others have done this too as a way to show thanks. I simply announce it on the most popular tribute page for the Saint.
http://saintexpedite.org/tribute.html

I am not affiliated with this site. I just know it is the most popular and will give Saint Expedite the Most attention.

My personal preference when thanking Saint Expedite:

I offer him 5 quarters which I then give to charity after a few days of letting them stay on the altar.

I offer 5 pieces of pound cake. After a few days I take the pound cake, break it up into crumbs inside of a plastic bag and go to the park and offer it to nature by sprinkling it on the ground.

I go to the website above and let people know that he has helped me. I am also doing this by publishing this book. I recently experienced wonderful miracles and promised Saint Expedite I would write this book as thanks.

And that is pretty much all there is to it.

ALTAR SETUP:

RED CANDLE

GLASS OF WATER   STATUE OF
                                  EXPEDITE

When he responds to your request, you may place the offerings in the middle of the altar between the 3 items above. It is not mandatory to have the candle lit when you make the offering, only during the ritual itself.

As you can see, it is not complicated, just a few things are required of you. In the next chapter we will essentially be doing the same ritual but with different prayers

Saint Expedite Magick - The Rituals

We will now go through a ritual to Saint Expedite. Now the ritual is pretty much the same, but we will be using different prayers for each one. **The prayers being used are not my own. I have quoted them verbatim from their respective sources. I will provide the links to the sites that I obtained them from.** You may also say your own prayers as well. My latest ritual used my own prayer. In either case, all of them work. I would pick the one that most resonates with you.

You will notice that many of the prayers seem rather demanding, this is okay, it is part of the tradition, you may temper these prayers if you like.

RITUAL 1 - To Remedy Dire Financial Needs

Steps:

Start this on a Wednesday if at all possible.

1. Setup the altar and light the candle

RED CANDLE

GLASS OF WATER

STATUE OF EXPEDITE

2. Say the following prayer:

"I call forth the Power and the presence of St. Expedite in my time of financial trouble. I offer my body, heart, mind and soul upon your altar of light. I have faith and trust and complete confidence that you will be my strength in this time of need. Quickly come to my assistance.

Bring to me _____ (Clearly express what you want, and ask him to find a way to get it to you.)

My financial need is urgent. Be my Light and Guide in this situation so that I may live with peace, love, prosperity and abundance and in the Praise of God.

Amen."

Prayer Sources: http://saintexpedite.org/prayers.html

Now make sure to state what you will give him in return for your request

This ritual should be done once a day at the very least. Please allow the candle to burn through. **But make sure you do not leave candles burning unattended.** If your request has not been fulfilled after the 7 day candle is out, please light a new one. Keep this going until St Expedite has fulfilled your request.

RITUAL 2 - To Remedy General Economic Problems

Steps:

Start this on a Wednesday if at all possible.

1. Setup the altar and light the candle

RED CANDLE

GLASS OF WATER

STATUE OF EXPEDITE

2. Say the following prayer:

I come before you, Saint Expedite,

To remedy economic problems in my work and my home.

And to ask for your powerful support.

Saint Expedite, protect my income,

That I may obtain sufficient money for necessities,

And tranquility and joy will reign in my house.

By your grace, Blessed Saint,

I request and pray that I will achieve my desire.

_____ (Clearly express what you want, and ask

him to find a way to get it to you.)

And I will give thanks for your glorious intercession.

Amen."

Prayer Sources: http://saintexpedite.org/prayers.html and http://www.luckymojo.com/saintexpedite.html

Now make sure to state what you will give him in return for your request

This ritual should be done once a day at the very least. Please allow the candle to burn through. **But make sure you do not leave candles burning unattended.** If your request has not been fulfilled after the 7 day candle is out, please light a new one. Keep this going until St Expedite has fulfilled your request.

RITUAL 3 - For Expedited Help

Steps:

Start this on a Wednesday if at all possible.

1. Setup the altar and light the candle

RED CANDLE

GLASS OF WATER   STATUE OF EXPEDITE

2. Say the following prayer:

Saint Expedite, you lay in rest.

I come to you and ask that this wish be granted.

_____ (Clearly express what you want, and ask

him to

find a way to get it to you.)

Expedite now what I ask of you.

Expedite now what I want of you, this very second.

Don't waste another day.

Grant me what I ask for.

I know your power, I know you because of your work.

I know you can help me.

Do this for me and I will spread your name with love and honor

so that it will be invoked again and again.

Expedite this wish with speed, love, honor, and goodness.

Glory to you, Saint Expedite! "

Prayer Sources: http://saintexpedite.org/prayers.html and
http://www.luckymojo.com/saintexpedite.html

**Now make sure to state what you will give him in return
for your request**

This ritual should be done once a day at the very least. Please allow the candle to burn through. **But make sure you do not leave candles burning unattended.** If your request has not been fulfilled after the 7 day candle is out, please light a new one. Keep this going until St Expedite has fulfilled your request.

RITUAL 4 - For Very Urgent Needs

Steps:

Start this on a Wednesday if at all possible.

1. Setup the altar and light the candle

RED CANDLE

GLASS OF WATER

STATUE OF EXPEDITE

2. Say the following prayer:

"Our dear martyr and protector, Saint Expedite,

You who know what is necessary and what is urgently

needed.

I beg you to intercede before the Holy Trinity, that by your

grace

my request will be granted.

_____ (Clearly express what you want, and ask

him to

find a way to get it to you.)

May I receive your blessings and favors.

In the name of our Lord Jesus Christ, Amen."

Prayer Sources: http://saintexpedite.org/prayers.html and http://www.luckymojo.com/saintexpedite.html

Now make sure to state what you will give him in return for your request

This ritual should be done once a day at the very least. Please allow the candle to burn through. **But make sure you do not leave candles burning unattended.** If your request has not been fulfilled after the 7 day candle is out, please light a new one. Keep this going until St Expedite has fulfilled your request.

RITUAL 5 - For Extra Quick actions

Steps:

Start this on a Wednesday if at all possible.

1. Setup the altar and light the candle

RED CANDLE

GLASS OF WATER   STATUE OF EXPEDITE

2. Say the following prayer:

" Saint Expedite,

Noble Roman youth, martyr,

You who quickly brings things to pass,

You who never delays, I come to you in need:

_____ (Clearly express what you want and ask him to

find a way to get it to you.)

Do this for me, Saint Expedite, and when it is

accomplished,

I will as rapidly reply with an offering to you.

(State your vow or promise)

Be quick, Saint Expedite!

Grant my wish before your candle burns out, and I will

glorify your name.

Amen".

**Now make sure to state what you will give him in return
for your request**

This ritual should be done once a day at the very least. Please

allow the candle to burn through. **But make sure you do not

leave candles burning unattended.** If your request has not

been fulfilled after the 7 day candle is out, please light a new

one. Keep this going until St Expedite has fulfilled your request.

RITUAL 6 - For Protection

Steps:

Start this on a Wednesday if at all possible.

1. Setup the altar and light the candle

RED CANDLE

GLASS OF WATER   STATUE OF
                                  EXPEDITE

2. Say the following prayer:

" St. Expedite honored by the gratitude of those who have invoked thee at the last hour and for pressing cases. We pray thee to obtain from the all-powerful goodness of God, by the intercession of Mary Immaculate, today, or such a day the grace we solicit with all submission to the Divine Will.".

Prayer Sources: http://saintexpedite.org/prayers.html

Now make sure to state what you will give him in return for your request

This ritual should be done once a day at the very least. Please allow the candle to burn through. **But make sure you do not leave candles burning unattended.** If your request has not been fulfilled after the 7 day candle is out, please light a new one. Keep this going until St Expedite has fulfilled your request.

The above rituals will work very well for you, but please remember to make the offerings you promised him. We discussed the kinds of offerings in the previous chapter. It is imperative that you do so because he will take everything back if you don't make the offering. Take Heed!

Extra Pieces of Advice - Please Read

In this chapter I will give you some general advice that will help enhance your rituals as well as give you additional information.

1. Some websites recommend that when you place his images on the altar, you should turn it upside down, supposedly this make St Expedite work faster. I WILL TELL YOU NOW, DO NOT DO THIS, ITS VERY DISRESPECTFUL

2. If at all possible, do celebrate his feast day on April 19th. It's a nice way to show reverence.

3. Keep candles lit until he grants your request. Make sure to be responsible, do not let candles burn when you are not home.

4. You may use incense in your rituals is you like. Any kind will do.

5. Read some of the tributes on http://saintexpedite.org/tribute.html it will enhance your faith.

6. Do Not do the ritual naked, at least cover your midsection.

7. **Focus on one request at a time.**

8. Do not ask St Expedite to do anything evil or harmful. HE WILL TURN IT ON YOU.

9. ALWAYS BE SURE TO GIVE HIM WHAT YOU PROMISED

10. Announce to the world either on the site I provided or other sites that Saint Expedite has fullfileld your request.

11. It is possible that St Expedite will not fulfill a given request. In the event that this is the case. DO NOT offer him an offering. He is a spirit of give and take. If you did not get benefit, do not give an offering.

Conclusion

This concludes Volume 2 of the Magick Of The Saints Series: The Magick of Saint Expedite. As you have seen, it is quite simple. There is no pomp and circumstance, no expensive ritual garments and paraphernalia, no odd and impossible herbs to obtain, no directions to turn to, no contrived and pompous terminology and phrases. Just pure, honest Magick using Saint Expedite. I am filled with utmost confidence that once you have preformed one of these rituals, you will enter a magickal partnership with the blessed saint. I would also like to say that the prayers mentioned are examples, if you like, you may use your own wording. In fact, I encourage you to do so.

Please note that it is okay for your to perform these rituals. It is not a sin and never will be. It is a divine and sacred art and will be forevermore.

Links Of Interest

I am not affiliated with any of these sites

http://saintexpedite.org/index.html

http://www.luckymojo.com/saintexpedite.html

http://miraclesfulfilled.blogspot.com/2013/07/saint-expedite-prayer-for-urgent-needs.html

http://saint-expedite.blogspot.com/

http://thedivinemercy.org/news/story.php?NID=5950

Other Books By The Author

The Mantra Magick Series:

VASHIKARAN MAGICK - LEARN THE DARK MANTRAS OF SUBJUGATION

Kali Mantra Magick: Summoning The Dark Powers of Kali Ma

Seed Mantra Magick: Master The Primordial Sounds of The universe

Chakra Mantra Magick: Tap Into The Magick Of Your Chakras

Tara Mantra Magick: How To Use The Power Of The Goddess Tara

Tibetan Mantra Magick: Tap Into The Power Of Tibetan Mantras

The Scared Names Series:

THE 72 NAMES OF GOD - THE 72 KEYS OF TRANSFORMATION

THE 72 ANGELS OF THE NAME - CALLING ON THE 72 ANGELS OF GOD

THE 99 NAMES OF ALLAH - ACQUIRING THE 99 DIVINE QUALITIES OF GOD

THE HIDDEN NAMES OF GENESIS - TAP INTO THE HIDDEN POWER OF MANIFESTATION

Magick Of the Saints Series

Ouija Board Magic Series

Crystal Magick Mantra Series

Supernatural Attainment Series

About the series

Magick of the Saints is a new series by bestselling Author Baal Kadmon. In this series we will discover the magical rites and powers of the saints. Many volumes are yet to be written. Please check back soon.

Below are the saints Baal Kadmon will be covering in this series but not necessarily in this order:

St. Anthony- finds lost items, keys, lovers

St. Joseph- pay raise, job getting, home affairs, home sales, passage to easier death

St. Barbara- protector of death and battles

St. Expedite- helps bring quick financial help

St. Christopher- protects travelers

St. Francis of Assisi- protects animals

St. Clare/Clair- guides one to wisdom and light

St. Raymond- protects against foes and gossipers

St. Ann- mothers, childbirth, grandmothers

Infant of Prague- protects children

St. Gerard- pregnancy, motherhood

St. Martha- protection, used to keep a man faithful

St. Jude- works impossible cases

Mary Magdalene-perfumers, penitent women, hairstylists, pharmacists, apothecaries

St. Peter- opens doors, businesses

St. Brigit- protects babies, children, travelers, scholars, sailors

St. Benedict- protector from witchcraft, illness, sickness, heals the sick

Our Lady of Guadalupe- the blessed virgin- blessings, love, healing, protection

St. George- soldiers, horsemen, defender, butchers, field workers, armourers, calvary

Holy Family- peace, loyalty, family

St. Helena- widows, divorcees, difficult marriages

St. Lucy- writers, poets, journalist

St. Sophia- wisdom, enlightenment, students

St. Michael the Archangel- an angel - used as protector from evil.

DISCLAIMER

Disclaimer: By law, I need to add this statement.

This volume of " Magick Of The Saints" is for educational purposes only and does not claim to prevent or cure any disease. The advice and methods in this book should not be construed as financial ,medical or psychological treatment. Please seek advice from a professional if you have serious financial, medical or psychological issues.

By purchasing , reading and or listening to this book, you understand that results are not guaranteed. In light of this, you understand that in the event that this book or audio does not work or causes harm in any area of your life, you agree that you do not hold Baal Kadmon, Amazon, its employees or affiliates liable for any damages you may experience or incur.

Printed in Great Britain
by Amazon